PATH CROSSINGS

Dr. Mark F. Horstemeyer

PATH CROSSINGS
Copyright© Dr. Mark F. Horstemeyer 2000

ISBN 0 75411 208 X

First published 2000 by
MINERVA PRESS
315-317 Regent Street
London W1R 7YB

Second printing 2005 by
Mississippi State University
Printing Services
Mississippi State, Mississippi

ABOUT THE AUTHOR

Mark F. Horstemeyer is a Chair Professor in Computational Solid Mechanics in Mechanical Engineering at Mississippi State University. He had worked at Sandia National Laboratories for fifteen years. He holds a Bachelor of Science from West Virginia University, a Master of Science from Ohio State University and Doctor of Philosophy from Georgia Institute of Technology, all in Mechanical Engineering. Dr. Horstemeyer has written over one hundred publications in the form of journal articles, conference proceedings and technical reports. He, his wife Barbara, his son Christopher, and his daughter Nicole reside in Starkville, Mississippi.

PREFACE

It is so easy to think about the significant events in life as being reserved for the rich and famous. Even as Christians, it is more often than not the norm for one to underrate his or her place in God's economy. In this book, the *anonymous* Christian is turned loose as a weapon in the hands of Almighty God; not a weapon of condemnation of the lost but a weapon of destruction against the strategies of hell, which are bent on ruining every human being's upward destiny.

In *Path Crossings* you will find your own life intersecting with that of strangers through the examples of Dr. Mark Horstemeyer's experiences... experiences that end up being anything but mundane. You will recognize the conversations of people very familiar to you, people who live all around you in your world of ups and downs, ins and outs. Hopefully, you will see the relative ease with which you can turn a simple and frivolous conversation into dialogue with eternal implications.

This book is at first glance just plain fun reading. Each story contains its own unique challenges and inevitable hopes. You will find yourself laughing and crying along with the players in each scenario. If you've never shared your faith as a Christian, you will see how easy and meaningful it is. If you've been taught that *witnessing* is a methodological bore, fasten your seatbelt for a new way of thinking. Bringing people closer to God, as Dr. Mark teaches it, is simply a matter of letting God unveil the circumstances of everyday life in such a way that you recognize them as a path crossing. And one thing I expect you will notice for sure is that bad things happen to good people so that other people can find the good God!

A book like this is overdue because it is not a treatise on the profundities of evangelism. Instead, it reads like a book of Acts for the 'average' Christian. As you read through these Spirit-filled pages may the same Holy Spirit who has blessed Dr. Mark time and again with an insight that moves a mundane moment to a divine blessing every moment of your life. May you recognize, more than ever, the amazing path crossings that God graciously allows you to participate in. May this book be one of those path crossings for you!

Ron Pinkston

CONTENTS

Introduction 9

The Jew 13

The Seeker 19

The Gentile. 23

The Family 31

The Storm. 37

The Scientist. 41

The Homosexual 47

The Sick. 53

Racism 57

Perspective. 61

The Religious. 65

Closure 71

INTRODUCTION

What is a path-crossing? In the story of Joseph in the book of Genesis, a path-crossing is clearly illustrated. Joseph was the youngest of his brothers. His father had sent him to find out the status of his brothers' efforts while shepherding a large flock of sheep. This was the beginning of a tortuous life-long journey for Joseph who ended up becoming second-in-command to Pharaoh ruling over Egypt. First, a string of important circumstances had to occur before Joseph could be placed in this high position by God. God orchestrated Joseph's life by weaving people in and out that deeply influenced him. One particular person is often overlooked by readers of this story of Joseph because he appears to be insignificant, but this person dramatically altered Joseph's course.

The story picks up in Genesis 37:14-17. And Israel said to Joseph, "Go and see if it is well with your brothers and with the flocks and bring me back a good word." Israel then sent Joseph out from the vale of Hebron to Shechem. And a certain man found him, because he (Joseph) was wondering in the field. The man asked him, "What are you seeking?" And Joseph answered, "I am seeking my brothers. Could you tell me where they are feeding the flocks?" And the man said, "They have departed from here but I heard them say that they were headed toward Dothan." Joseph continued after his brothers and found them in Dothan. Just after he found them, his brothers sold him to the Ishamaelites.

Let's consider this unnamed traveler who directed Joseph to his brothers. First, there was a plan for Joseph set out by his father. In trying to fulfill that plan, Joseph found himself wandering and not knowing where to go. At this critical time, the unnamed man enters the scene and directs Joseph along the right path. Joseph headed aimlessly down a certain road, but because the unnamed man crossed his path, Joseph's life was forever changed. This exemplifies a path-crossing.

Similar to this wonderful plan that God had for Joseph, He has a wonderful plan for every person. Like Joseph's father, God lays out the plan, but like Joseph, we go astray and start wandering from the path that God designed. This is why God will send somebody to cross our path. The goal: to redirect us toward the God-ordained path. The goal is accomplished with more information being revealed about God and His truth. That is what the unnamed man did with Joseph and that is what God wants us to do with those whom He ordains to cross our paths.

A path-crossing is like an equation with three components. The first component is the "giver" of information: it is the responsibility of the giver to recognize the path-crossing and share God's truth. The second component is the "receiver" of the information: it is the responsibility of the receiver to obey the truth. The third component is God: it is God's responsibility to set up the meeting and reveal the essence of the meeting to both the giver and receiver.

Sometimes we are the receiver, and sometimes we are the giver. Sharing information to help redirect somebody's path toward their God-planned destiny is something crucial to remember. God didn't call us to change anybody or their path. However, He did command us to proclaim the truth. It is the receiver's responsibility to act on the information given.

There is a stream of people that God will run across your path in life. Before you had a relationship with the Lord, He sent many people across your path to reveal more and more of Himself. In general, before a clear enough picture results to make a decision to follow Christ, several encounters with God's representatives are often needed. Wouldn't it be nice to know at the end of your life that the people who crossed your path were redirected towards God, and maybe even so much so that their lives were completely changed because of an encounter with God through you?

Each type of "path-crossing" can be different: some are repeat crossings while others will be just one time. Joseph met the unnamed traveler only once, and scriptures do not mention the traveler again. God designed certain people to be in our family and close to us for life. Others are friends, neighbors, or co-workers who will be with us for a season in our life. And then there are the strangers that we may see only once in our life.

In terms of the three component path-crossing equation, this book is written from the perspective of the "giver" of information. Although a book could be written to God's glory that would focus on the "receiving" of God's direction, this one is written to encourage you to be a giver just as you have received. Sharing the love that Jesus Christ has shared with you in a path-crossing is a blessing that we often miss or neglect. Many times God has set up divine appointments in our lives, and we don't recognize them as such, but when we do, something of permanence occurs. I have experienced that in my own life, which is why I am writing this book. In particular, I share some of the path-crossings that I experienced with a broad range of people while traveling by airplane across the United States. In many of the path-crossings, the "receiver" did not accept the Lord as his/her savior, but they received the truth of God's love and more information so that their path could be redirected towards God. Hopefully, you will gather some insight about some of the "types" of "receivers" as you read this book, for example, a Jew or Gentile. I have also woven the story of Joseph throughout the book as an example of how God has woven path-crossings not only through-out Joseph's life but mine and yours as well.

It is amazing how God organizes a meeting between two individuals for His sovereign purpose. God has done that with me many times on an airplane. That is one of my favorite places to meet new people. Yours may not be on an airplane but at the local laundry facility, at the ballpark, at the library, or at your workplace. Where-ever you are, people are around you at some point during your day. Take some time to think about who is around you in your day. These are the people that God has chosen to cross your path. A reason exists for these path-crossings. It is that God wants you to show them something about Him. You are His ambassador. You know Him, and now He wants them to know Him. So I want to encourage you in whatever place you are, someone is near you that could use a touch of God's hand. As a matter of fact, it's often just a realization that God has run a person across your path for His divine purposes so that you can introduce that person to Jesus. He wants to use you in their processing.

Indeed, a process of continual communications from God to an individual occurs even before a relationship with Jesus starts. If you remember in your own life before you came into the understanding of God's love, God gave you different unctions of His unseen presence in various forms and manners. It took awhile for you to understand until finally the light turned on, and then you gave your life to the Lordship of Jesus Christ. Now God, in turn, uses us as part of the process for someone else to come into a relationship with Him. I have heard it said that Jesus must be introduced to someone seven times before they would give their heart over to Him. Obviously, that is not true for everyone, but this saying can teach the "giver" patience in sharing the Gospel. Seven times seems like a lot considering that some people will make friendships after only the first meeting. But a relationship with God takes more meetings, because we are talking about a friend of whom we relate to not by our senses but our spirit. Many times we are so caught up the busyness of our day that we miss the opportunity of the path-crossings that God has ordained. Yet a great potential well of joy exists that we can experience if we don't focus on **my** life, or **my** job, or **my** family.

I pray that as you read this book that God's joy will fill you with new revelation about how God uses path-crossings in your life. I also pray that God will paint a vision in your mind that you can be used by Him. Throughout this book remember that my airplane may be a dinner table, a bus, the desk at your office, or your front yard.

I should also note in the following stories, the names of the people have been changed for confidential purposes.

Chapter 1 "The Jew"

Romans 9:3-4 For I could wish that myself were accursed from Christ for my brethren, my kinsmen according to the flesh: who are Israelites; to whom pertain the adoption, the glory, the covenants, the giving of the law, the service of God, and the promises. (KJV)

The apostle Paul penned the words of Romans 9:3-4 to show his affection for the unsaved Jew. He knew of the rich heritage that the Jews had. He was one. He was raised in a Jewish family. He was part of the Jewish Sanhedrin, the religious leadership of the day. Then something dramatic occurred. Jesus interrupted Paul's life by abruptly stopping him on a trip to Damascus. A brilliant light shined that blinded Paul. In the midst of the light, the Lord spoke to Paul about direction for his life. Paul's course was dramatically changed indeed.

Jesus also interrupted the life of a Jewish friend of mine, but in a much less dramatic way. On a flight from Albuquerque, New Mexico to Oakland, California, (many of us who work for Sandia National Laboratories travel this route because the mother part of the company is in Albuquerque), I experienced a path-crossing. I was the first to sit down in my row. After a few minutes, another gentleman, whom I knew from working at Sandia at the California site, sat down next to me. This was unusual. I don't remember being seated next to someone on a plane that worked with my company unless I planned it ahead of time. We greeted each other politely with the mutual appreciation that we recognized each other although we hadn't been formally introduced. This was our opportunity to get to know each other. I had seen him in meetings before but from a distance. This path-crossing was our first and thank God I recognized it as such.

Dan was middle-aged, well-educated, married, and had three

boys. The youngest son, then in high school, was causing intense family problems. During our discussion about this troubling situation, Dan mentioned that his Jewish faith was helping him during this trial. Dan mentioned God in terms of a Higher Power. I took this as an opportunity to share about my relationship with his Messiah, Jesus the Christ. The key to leading a Jew to Christ is to appeal to their knowledge of the Old Testament and then show them how it points to Jesus.

I mentioned to Dan that in his Torah, the Isaiah prophesied about Jesus some 600 years in advance. And that Isaiah's prophecies were confirmed by the Dead Sea Scrolls. In one particular scripture, Jesus is clearly portrayed as the suffering messiah who understands our pain and grief.

Isaiah 53:3-12 He is despised and rejected of men; a man of sorrows, and acquainted with grief: and we hid as it were our faces from him; he was despised, and we esteemed him not. Surely he has born our griefs and carried our sorrows; yet we did esteem him stricken, smitten of God and afflicted. But he was wounded for our transgressions, he was bruised for our iniquities: the chastisement of our peace was upon him; and with his stripes we are healed. All we like sheep have gone astray, we have turned every one to his own way; and the Lord has laid on him the iniquity of us all. He was oppressed, and he was afflicted, yet he opened not his mouth; he is brought as a lamb to the slaughter, as a sheep before her shearers is dumb, so he opened not his mouth. He was taken from prison and from judgment: and who shall declare his generation: for he was cut off out of the land of the living: for the transgression of my people was he stricken. And he made his grave with the wicked, and with the rich in his death; because he had done no violence, neither was any deceit in his mouth. Yet it pleased the Lord to bruise him; he has put him to grief: when you shall make his soul an offering for sin, he shall see his seed, he shall prolong his days, and the pleasure of the Lord shall prosper in his hand. He shall see of the travail of his soul, and shall be satisfied: by his knowledge shall my righteous servant justify many; for he shall bear their iniquities. Therefore will I divide him a portion with the great, and he shall divide the spoil with the strong; because he has poured out his soul unto death; and he was numbered with the transgressors; and he bare the sin of many, and made intercession for the transgressors. (KJV)

Dan smiled and listened to me as I shared about the Jewish messianic prophecies, but I knew that he wasn't getting the point. It seemed that blinders were on his eyes. His eyes were physically opened, but I could tell that he was not catching the full impact of this passage. He was even trying to understand, asking many questions, but he just could not comprehend what the coming of the Messiah, Jesus, meant. He acknowledged that the Messiah would demonstrate the attributes mentioned in the Isaiah passage, but he would not agree that it was referring to Jesus.

I remember one of the main issues to Dan was that he would not be Jewish anymore if he accepted Jesus as the Messiah. I had heard this argument before from other Jews. In fact, I had taken Hebrew at college from a Rabbi who told me that if he would become a Christian, he would no longer be a Jew, and he would also lose his job.

I tried to address Dan's concern about losing his Jewishness. "Dan, that is not true. By receiving Jesus into your heart, you are completing your Jewishness. All of the prophets who foretold of the Messiah were Jewish. Jesus was Jewish. All of the first-generation disciples of Jesus were Jews. The apostle Paul who wrote most of the New Testament was Jewish. Believing in Jesus as your Messiah completes the picture of the Jewish belief system."

I paused and then continued, "Although the Jewish religion all by itself is rich in tradition and appealing for its ritual and history, it lacks the assurance of eternal destiny because the main point, the Messiah, is still missing. I truly believe that by receiving Jesus into your heart as Messiah, you are completing your Jewishness as God intended."

"Mark, Christians don't believe that. Christians over the centuries have persecuted the Jews. Hitler proclaimed to be devout Roman Catholic. During the crusades, when the Christians fought against the Islamic people, they also persecuted the Jews. "

"There is something here that is critical to understand, Dan. By performing religious ceremony doesn't mean you are a Christian. Just because people go to church doesn't mean that they are a Christian. These people claimed to be Christians, but to be a Christian is one where your life is surrendered to the Lordship of Jesus Christ. I don't think that Hitler was surrendered to the Lordship of Jesus Christ nor do I think were the leaders of the Crusade Wars. Today, there are people who claim to be Christians but are very different from the way that the Bible defines a Christian."

Dan conceded on this point, but he still did not understand that Jesus fulfilled the biblical prophecies as the Messiah. He also did not understand the need to accept Jesus as his savior. Amazingly though, Dan, did talk about his new understanding of releasing his anxiety and fear to a Higher Power, because of some circumstances with his wayward son. He also admitted how he had neglected his teenage son over the years. He further confessed the harm he caused by his domineering ways. His confessions were emotional and heartfelt. There was a sense of cleansing for him as he confessed his sins to me.

During our conversation, out of the corner of my eye I caught a glimpse of the person sitting in front of us. He was grumbling something about these religious fanatics behind him. He had enough and was about to move to another seat. I looked back at Dan. He was oblivious. He continued to share his pain and hurt over this situation with his son. I prayed under my breath for both Dan and the guy who listened to this two hour conversation.

Looking back, I realized that God organized a three way path crossing during that flight: one was Dan, the hurting Jew, another was the obstinate atheist sitting in front of us, and the third person was me. God destined for Dan to sit next to me and for both of us to sit behind the other man. I don't know where I fit into the process of both of them coming to know Jesus. Perhaps I was the first encounter for both of them. I have seen Dan off and on at work since that time, and we have shared more about our lives since then. As far as the atheist in front of us, I have never seen him again. Although neither man acknowledged Christ on that trip, I know that God spoke clearly to them through me and will bring others across their path to reconfirm His love for them. If He has to, He may even go Himself as He did for Paul on the road to Damascus.

Chapter 2 "The Seeker"

Jeremiah 29:13 and you shall seek me and find me when you search for me with all your heart. (KJV)

One of the most interesting path-crossings that I had ever experienced was on a trip from Los Angeles to Baltimore. Because of the nature of the upcoming business meeting, I planned to prepare for my presentation by reading a few journal articles on the plane. I had no intention of watching the movie or talking with the people next to me. Apparently, the Lord had other plans.

My journal articles were out and ready to read. As I started to read, I noticed a middle-aged woman settle in next to me. We exchanged hellos as she sat down, and I continued my reading. Something seemed wrong. *She said hello and gave me a pleasant smile, but something was unsettling about her countenance.*

I continued my reading, but was distracted with my traveling neighbor. The distraction was not anything that she had done or said nor was it any peculiar clothing. It was something in my heart that kept trying to arrest my attention. I finally recognized that God was trying to speak to me. At this point I knew that I may have to change my plans, because God wanted to use me in this lady's life.

I took a reading break shortly after we were in the air, and I noticed that she was reading a book entitled *When Bad Things Happen to Good People*. It was becoming clearer that this lady was hurting and God wanted our paths to cross. I have since forgotten her name, but I haven't forgotten what she told me next as we caught each other's attention.

Having heard of that book though never having read it, I asked, "Is that a good book?"

"Yes, it's helping me deal with some issues in my life."

She paused, took a deep breath, and then continued, "This past year I lost my husband."

"I am sorry to hear that."

"My son and I have had a difficult time adjusting to his loss and to some other things that have happened to us." She paused and then continued, "Do you remember when that USAIR plane crashed at the Los Angeles airport not too long ago?"

"Yes, weren't there two planes involved?"

"Yes. Well. My husband was the pilot of the bigger plane, and he didn't make it. I had to deal with a lot of anger and bitterness, because the air traffic controller, who caused the crash, was incompetent. It wasn't really his fault. I wasn't mad at him. He had mental problems. I was mad at the people who hired him. They should have known that the controller had mental problems. That's who I am bitter at. I guess my bitterness has subsided a bit. I am just realizing this as I talk with you. I have not talked to many people about this." And then looking into the air she said, "And here I am telling this to a stranger."

She continued, "That hasn't been the most troubling part though."

It's not? What could be worse than this?! I thought.

"My husband's family is blaming me for his death. And they have alienated my son and me from their family. It has gotten so bad that we had to move and not let them know where we are living."

In utter astonishment I asked gently, "How can they blame you for your husband's death?"

She broke down with tears and offered, "I don't know."

I turned to the Lord in silent prayer. *Lord, what can I do to help this lady? She has big troubles that I cannot address. I sensed an immediate leading from the Lord. There were two things I needed to do: (1) listen to her with empathy, and (2) tell her about God's love and acceptance of her.*

"I am sorry about this situation that you are in. If I may be frank with you, I don't think that your husband's death was your fault. I also think that your husband's family is out-of-line for mistreating you and your son in this manner. It is hard enough to grieve his loss and deal with the bitterness and anger of the situation, let alone get blamed for it."

This opened the floodgate of thoughts for her. She spoke her mind for quite a while as I just sat and actively listened. At the end of her emotionally driven words about what had happened, she mentioned that a friend had given her this book. She said that while she was reading this book she was somewhat encouraged but still felt distant from God. She claimed to not have the closeness that these people in this book had experienced. She knew something was missing but didn't know what it was.

"Do you know that God dearly loves you? It may not appear that way but if you can believe that the Lord loves you and accepts you, you will realize that what Satan means for bad, God will turn for good."

"I want to believe it, but I don't feel that way."

"Have you ever prayed to give your life over to Jesus Christ? You see, from the beginning of creation, God designed men and women to have a void in their lives that only He could fill. He designed this void because of His love. He knows that only true love can come from God so when we allow Him to fill the void and accept His love, then we understand and feel the love and acceptance of God. We also then have the capacity to love others as God has loved us. Adam and Eve fell from their relationship with God, because of their disobedience to Him, but Jesus came to restore that relationship by dying on the cross and rising from the dead for us so that we can have abundant life. What it takes on our part is giving up our lives in exchange for His life. The Bible calls this repentance."

I could tell that she had never fully repented, where she totally asked God to forgive her of her sins and give her life totally over to His control. I could tell from her look that she had thought she was a Christian but never gave her life over to God.

I continued, "It doesn't matter if you have gone to church all your life. Going to church makes you a Christian as much as going to Wendy's makes you a hamburger. Being a Christian is a second-by-second experience in which you have fellowship in a loving relationship with Jesus Christ." Something seemed to click-on.

"I want this relationship."

"You can have it. It is a gift from God." I continued, "Pray after me. Lord, forgive me of my sins."

"Forgive me of my sins."

"Give me hope about my life and my son's life," She repeated.

"Help me to forgive those who have treated me badly and wrongly." She and I continued for several minutes until I sensed the completion of the prayer. We looked at each other, and I could almost hear the angels in heaven rejoicing over this lady. We continued talking as I could see her burden lifted from her. She now understood and felt the inner peace of God. She was encouraged and free.

I have not heard from her since our path-crossing, but I did send her some information to encourage her in her relationship with the Lord.

Some appointments of divine destiny occur, and we are not aware of them occurring as they happen. I became aware of God's presence and the plan of this particular path-crossing after I gave up my plans for study. This kind of opportunity awaits us many times, but we often miss it. We are so into **our** schedule, **our** plans, and **our** lives that we miss God's plan. God many times sends people across our paths so that He can shower His love upon them through us. More often than not, these people are more willing to hear than we are to speak. There are so many people searching for answers, yet the answers may not be obvious for some reason in their search. And God wants to use us to clarify the answers for them.

I could have ignored this person next to me and went about my own business. If I did, I would have missed a blessing for me and, more importantly, salvation for her.

Chapter 3 "The Gentile"

Acts 11:17-18 Forasmuch then as God gave them the like gift as he did unto us, who believed on the Lord Jesus Christ; what was I, that I could withstand God? When they heard these things, they held their peace, and glorified God, saying, Then hath God also to the Gentiles granted repentance unto life. (KJV)

The context of this passage of scripture is extremely important. Never before did a Jew think that God would bestow his blessing upon a Gentile, that is, anybody who is not Jewish. God had chosen the Jewish nation to be His blessed people. The New Testament reveals so clearly that God desires to shed His grace upon all people, Jew and Gentile alike. In this biblical text, God had to show Peter, who was steeped in Jewish religion and culture, that God's plan was bigger that Peter's religious and cultural frame of reference. God wanted to reach out to the first century Gentiles through Peter. In a similar vein, God wanted to reach out to an ancient Egyptian Pharoah through Joseph.

Joseph had been in jail after being falsely accused of raping the Potiphar's wife. While in jail, he interpreted dreams for two people: a baker and the chief cupbearer of the Pharaoh. The interpretation of the cupbearer's dream was to bring him deliverance from his jail cell in three days. The cupbearer was grateful for this interpretation and promised to tell the Pharaoh once he got out of jail but forgot. Two years later, the pharaoh had a dream and nobody could interpret it. At this time, the cupbearer remembered Joseph and told of how Joseph interpreted his dream and that of the baker. Pharaoh ordered that Joseph be brought before his presence. In front of Pharoah, Joseph interpreted the dream which eventually saved Egypt from a great famine. It also allowed the Pharaoh to become the most powerful leader on earth at the time.

I am amazed that God gave this dream to Pharaoh. It was a blessed dream. God wanted not only Joseph to come out of jail, but he wanted to bless this world leader. Pharaoh was not a Jew. He was not one of the lineage of the promised Messiah, yet God chose to bless and prosper him. God raises and lowers men to places of power, and he chose in this instance to reach out to this Gentile, who in turn would bless His people. We understand that God reached out to the first century Jews through the Apostle Peter. Sometimes we forget that He reached out to the Gentiles long before Christ like He did to this Pharaoh through Joseph. He also wants to reach out to the Gentiles of our day.

On a flight from Washington D.C. to San Francisco, a divine appointment was set up with a "Gentile" whom I worked with, Anthony. We had been working on a military missile project together. We were feeling good about our work as we were traveling back from the first successful test of the largest experimental weapon's program in history.

Anthony grew up in the Roman Catholic Church but professed to be agnostic. An agnostic is one who admits that there could be a God, but won't admit that there is one. In other words, it was possible for God to exist, but probably is not likely. It is an intellectually satisfying position because agnostics don't have to admit that they are atheists. To be an atheist is to believe that no God exists. This implies that you know everything to say that no God exists. An agnostic lives like no God exists, but you don't have admit that he doesn't. Anthony and I traveled quite a bit together but never had the opportunity to discuss "spiritual" things, that is, until this trip.

It was obvious that Anthony's heart was hardened from the religiosity of the church. There was no softness towards God. He grew up seeing the hypocritical lifestyles of those in the church claiming to be Christians. This bothered him. He not only saw this in the Catholic Church but in other churches he visited while growing up. He concluded it was the same throughout Christendom: no genuine religious experience within the people, just an outward show. As a result, through his scientific training he developed an evolutionary based belief system.

His belief allowed for God to exist but also allow him to live like He does not exist. This is the stance of the agnostic.

I had to meet Anthony where he was spiritually at and deal with the walls that he raised because of his religious experience.

Because I grew up in a "religious" church similar to Anthony's, I felt that I could identify with him a bit. In the midst of our conversation, I shared how I came into an intimate relationship with the Lord Jesus Christ. It went like this.

"Look Anthony, I grew up in a similar environment as you. I went to church every Sunday. I saw people claiming to be Christians, acting like one on Sunday, and living however they wanted the rest of the week. I lost respect for Christians. I even lost respect for the pastor. I asked him how I could get to heaven. He said that nobody really knew how to get to heaven. I gave up on the Church at that point.

It wasn't until several years later that I came full circle at age 17 with that question, but this time it was with my brother Stephen and a friend, Russell, who had recently experienced the very real presence of God. Since then, I have come to realize what heaven really is ... being continually in the presence of God. These two guys had an experience related to my question about how to get to heaven. They were experiencing some of heaven on earth. From the time that I had asked the pastor about how to get to heaven until I talked with my brother and friend, I had gone through some difficult teenage years."

I paused to gage Anthony's attention. He seemed to be tracking with me, so I continued, "At first, I was trying to find my identity. I wondered why I was born into the Horstemeyer family. I didn't choose that; it just happened to me. Why wasn't I living during George Washington's time? How come I was living on this block with these other kids? There had to be a reason. There had to be a purpose for my life. What was it? What was my identity? Who was I? These questions perplexed me. I didn't constantly think about these questions, but they would come up here and there.

I thought that if I could be the best basketball player in my high school then I would be somebody important and that would be my identity. I wanted to be next Jerry West from West Virginia. After spending many hours practicing shooting, dribbling, and rebounding basketballs, I realized that I wasn't going to be the next Jerry West. Worse, I wasn't even going to be the best player on my high school team.

I then felt that an academic route was the best direction for my life. I had good grades, almost all A's. I joined different academic societies in my high school, only to find that all these people had problems too, many of them worse than me. Trying to find myself in the intellectual realm came up empty.

Next were alcohol, marijuana, and rock-n-roll. I typically would go out with my friends or brothers to rock concerts, and inevitably we would be drinking beer, whiskey, and wine. It wasn't long until we started to smoke marijuana and try cocaine. At this point, I was afraid I was loosing control.

Then I started running six to eight miles every day. This exertion allowed some relief to my aching, wandering heart, but there was still no lasting fulfillment. I always needed more.

Nothing I tried seemed to satisfy."

I sensed that Anthony wanted to hear me out.

"At one point, I almost committed suicide. I was standing over a bridge during one of my jogging excursions and pondered the thoughts of suicide. If I had no purpose, this was a logical end. Why was I here? No answers. Who am I? Again, no answers. If I killed myself, then I would be labeled as that crazy Mark Horstemeyer who couldn't deal with life. On the other hand, if I didn't commit suicide I would continue to go through life with all these unanswered problems. But there had to be an answer. There had to be a reason for living. I was popular with all the different crowds: drug crowd, sports crowd, and academic crowd. Yet none of those things satisfied. Something didn't make sense with all this. There had to be meaning to life. There just had to be purpose. There must be something else that I haven't tried yet that would give me the answer, and I am going to find it. That was the essence of my thought patterns during that time period of my life.

I was searching for God and didn't even know it. Looking back, I see now that everybody goes through something like this in their life. There is a good reason for it too: God designed us with a void deep within our being that only He can fill. There is a place in every human's heart for God to take residence. When we give Him that place of residence, we get peace ... perfect peace, knowing that we are at peace with our Creator. Until we allow Him to take residence in our heart, we have unrest, or lack of peace. By this lack of peace, we have troubles identifying the problem. We only know that something within us is not right. That's when the search starts. We may not be cognizant that we are even searching for something; it may manifest itself in different forms. I didn't recognize that I was searching for anything. I just felt driven."

Anthony responded, "I think that everyone goes through something like that in their lives at sometime but it always seems to work itself out."

I retorted, "Not for everyone, Anthony. Unfortunately, I personally know some people who have committed suicide. And I was close friends with them. Fortunately for me, I came to recognize the God-void in my life."

"It wasn't long after this black period in my life that my brother Stephen stopped taking drugs and drinking beer. I asked him, 'Stephen, what happened.'"

"Stephen said, 'Jesus Christ is real, and He is coming back soon. As a matter of fact, Jesus is coming so soon that I want to be ready to meet Him. This is why I stopped all the drinking and smoking.'

I smirked at him. Outside I scoffed, but inside I had a spark of hope. *But I tried this God thing*, I thought. That's what got me started on this other stuff.

'Did you know that the pastor told me that we can't know if we will ever make it to heaven?' I asked Stephen.

'I'm not talking about church or religion. I'm talking about a relationship with Jesus Christ,' he proclaimed as he appeared to stare into my soul.

Stephen continued, 'Russell and I have been having Bible studies together and are going to a Bible study at church on Wednesday nights.'

I thought that he was leading me on, so I thought I would surprise him, 'I would like to go to your study with Russell.'

To my amazement, Stephen said that he and Russell weren't ready. After a couple of weeks of preparation, he came back and said that they were ready for me now."

"Anthony, I can remember it so vividly. I remember sitting with them on an early summer evening. Across the way, the little league games were going on. The humidity was still heavy in the warm air. The hope that sparked several weeks earlier was now beginning to grow. Russell opened up his Bible to the book of Daniel. He and Stephen read through several chapters, and then they started to illustrate a few points. I had never heard anything like this before in my life. It was rather weird. I had gone to church all my life, every Sunday that I could remember, and had **NEVER** heard of this before. It made me wonder how much I didn't know. They talked about how the Bible is full of predictive prophecy to prove its validity. They also said that Jesus is coming back, and if we don't have a personal relationship with Him, we will be left behind. We finished that night by them inviting me to come to the Wednesday night Bible study. I decided to go along.

I don't remember if it was my first or second time at the Bible study, but I will always remember what happened that night. When the study was over, I noticed that Stephen and Russell were headed upstairs to the sanctuary with several others as everybody else was leaving. The several others being Russell's mom and two other ladies. Nobody said anything to me, and it was a few seconds before I realized where they were going. As I walked behind by several yards, I saw that one of the ladies knelt down with the others surrounding her and praying for her. I had never seen anything like this. I thought, *I don't understand what is going on here,* but something in my heart was saying that this was okay. When they were finished, Russell's mom looked at me asked if I was ready. I didn't know what for, but I was ready for something.

As I walked toward that large white cross in front of the altar, I imagined Jesus on that cross. I knelt down just underneath it. I had seen that large white cross many times, but never really imagined what Jesus went through while on the cross. More importantly, I didn't realize the fullness of why he went to the cross. Now it was striking me like a lightning bolt. Everybody put their hands on my shoulders to pray.

I asked, 'What do I do?'

Russell responded, 'You need to give your life to God and ask Him to forgive you of your wrong doings. God will give you a new start, Mark.'

That was it! I needed a new start, where everything that I had done would be forgotten... then I could start over. I would be born again. I would have a new beginning. I would have a new identity; it would be in God through Jesus Christ. This was the salvation that I was looking for and didn't really know it until I was sitting under the cross.

With genuine respect for God, I asked, "God, forgive me of my sins and give me a new start.'

Anthony, I felt a warmth on the inside, a warmth that said I was at peace with my Creator. I had an overwhelming sense of satisfaction. Instantly, I knew that God accepted me, and I could accept myself. Instantly, I knew that I had purpose. I now understood that God made me and placed me in the Horstemeyer family. He designed for me to have three brothers. He created me with certain looks and various desires. I knew that He designed me. I had an excited hope about living. Now, life could be fully realized. I had a new lease on life.

The next Friday with a beer in my hand, I thought, *what am I doing this for. I'm already high on Jesus. Why do I want to come 'down' by drinking?* That night I made a vow to God never to drink alcohol again. I was free and didn't want to be in bondage again. This new found liberty made me so emotionally high that no drug, rock concert, or any drink could get me higher. Plus it was free, no strings attached. Furthermore, I didn't have to come down from this high. This Gentile (me) had come to know the saving grace of the Lord Jesus Christ."

There was another Gentile I was interested in now. Anthony listened intently the whole time and then started asking questions. First, about some of the details of my coming to know Jesus in an intimate way, and second about how my faith related to work in a practical way.

Suddenly, in the midst of our intense discussion, we felt the plane abruptly jerk. Earlier on our trip we had discussed the plane crash in Iowa where many died just several weeks before. With our technical background, we discussed the probability of another plane crash and concluded that it was still much safer to fly than drive a car. This sudden jerk quickly brought those thoughts back to our minds inducing an abrupt adrenaline shot through our veins.

It may have hit Anthony harder than me, because his quick and sudden response was "Mark! quick! Spit on me! Baptize me! Do something! We're crashing!"

My instant thought was *its too late for that*. Then simultaneously, just as suddenly as we felt that tremendous jerk, we both realized that we were just landing and the abrupt jerk was the plane having a rough landing. We were just landing, that's all.

We were so enthralled in our discussion that we lost track of time and didn't realize that we were so close to the San Francisco Airport. Instantly, Anthony felt embarrassed and tried to gain his composure. He didn't say a word. I was speechless too. We just looked at each other for a second. My look was one of seriousness. *Anthony, you just faced eternity and your true feelings came out. If we did wreck, it would have been too late. Let's do something about it now before it is really too late.*

He looked at me with an embarrassed smile, but I could tell that he had gone back into a comfort zone as if to say now that I know I am not going to die, I have no need for God.

Unfortunately to this day, Anthony has not given his life to Jesus Christ. I work just down the hall from him and talk with him occasionally about work. The Lord still wants me to share His love with Anthony, but even if I hint about talking about God, Anthony quickly changes the subject. It's too bad. Not for me, but for Anthony. We had a major path-crossing that day on the flight to San Francisco. There truly are no atheists in foxholes. It's too bad when some people get out of the foxhole, their flimsy faith retreats, and they go about acting as if God doesn't exist.

Chapter 4 "The Family"

Gen 45:1-2 *Then Joseph could not control himself before all those who stood by him, and he cried, "Have everyone go out from me." So there was no man with him when Joseph made himself known to his brothers. And he wept so loudly that the Egyptians heard it, and the household of Pharaoh heard it. (KJV)*

Joseph was second in command to the pharaoh of Egypt, the most powerful nation at the time in terms of power, economy, and influence. His work was important but not the most important thing to him. Most important was his God and then his family. Joseph had been betrayed by his brothers before given this great leadership position. When he saw his brothers again, he didn't respond with bitterness and unforgiveness, but with love, compassion, and gratefulness, because he was able to see them again.

We live in a day and age where many of us have moved from the place of our upbringing. As a result, our kids are often raised apart from their grandparents, aunts and uncles, and cousins. This has raised a personal internal conflict in my life and I am aware of it in others as well. My children won't experience the daily benefits of loving family members other than their immediate siblings and parents. Our society has rationalized this dilemma by claiming that our jobs demand us to move to other locations. This may be true for some and maybe even for most, but there are some who "sacrifice" the good job for another in order to be close to their family again. They deeply value their family. Joseph was a biblical example of one who highly esteemed his family. So did the man that I met on a flight from St. Louis to Washington D.C.

St. Louis airport was bustling with people. I had never seen it this crowded. I was hurrying along to reach my connecting flight to Washington D.C. since my flight out of San Francisco had arrived late.

As I arrived at the departing gate in St. Louis, I saw long lines at the counter for people checking in and for people boarding the plane. I would typically step into the boarding line onto the plane, because my ticket was checked at San Francisco, but I felt an inner, gentle sense that I should try to get an upgrade. So I stepped into the line at the counter to check-in.

This gentle urging had happened many times before, and I have come to realize that this is one of the ways that the Lord speaks to people. It is an inner leading of the heart, not the head. When I got to the counter, I applied for the upgrade by using some frequent flyer passes, but the ticket agent assured me that all of the first class seats were taken. Regardless, she would put me on the upgrade waiting list anyway. She told me not to enter the plane and after the others boarded the plane, she would know if a first class seat was available. After the announcer made final boarding call, the ticket agent directed me to go ahead and board the plane to my normal seat which was in row 22.

At this point I thought *Oh well, I guess that wasn't the Lord speaking to me after all.* I settled into my seat preparing for the three hour flight to Washington D.C. Just before they pushed the plane back to taxi to the runway, my name was called on the loudspeaker. I immediately knew that they were going to move me to the first class seat and I thought, *God really wants me to meet somebody up there in first class.*

As I sat down in row 2d, I observed the man who was just a few years older than me sitting in 2e. He was about six feet tall and had a quiet reserve about him. He was engrossed in his reading of what looked like technical papers and memos. I looked for opportunities to break into his world, but there just didn't seem to be any openings. Although I am not shy, I generally don't butt into somebody else's business unless there is some verbal or nonverbal communication to do so. Just before lunch, he put away his work, and I put away mine.

After exchanging smiles I introduced myself, "Hi! I'm Mark."

"Hello! I'm John. Are you from the D.C. area?"

"No, I'm from the San Francisco Bay area in a little town called Livermore."

"Oh, I know about Livermore. That's where Lawrence Livermore National Lab is."

"Yes, that's right. I work at Sandia National Labs in Livermore."

John with a quizzical look asked, "I thought Sandia Labs were in Albuquerque, New Mexico?"

I smiled, "You're right again, but we have a lab in Livermore as well. Many people don't know that. Even people who live in Livermore. Where do you work?"

"I work for an undersecretary who oversees environmental issues for our government," John replied.

"Whom does the undersecretary work for?"

"Vice President, Al Gore."

"Wow, that's a great opportunity."

John wasn't as impressed as I was about his job. To me he had a fairly high ranking position in our government, but I sensed in John's tone of voice that something was bothering him. Recalling the inner sense that I had previously from the Lord, I was searching for what the Lord wanted me to do or to say to this man.

He applied for the job but he didn't tell me why? In trying to see what the Lord wanted, I decided to ask more questions, but he beat me to the punch.

"I am aware of some of the things that Sandia does. We have had some Sandians on our working groups which oversee different environmental issues throughout the US. What do you do?"

I knew that we didn't have much time left on our flight, and I didn't want to get wrapped up in my work. I knew that God wanted me to minister to this guy. But how? I had to respond to the his questions though. I just blurted out, "I work in the area of mathematical modeling of high strain rate material behavior, like cars crashing or trains crashing. The notion is to simulate the crashes on the computer first in many different scenarios so that you don't have to experimentally wreck twenty cars. It's much less expensive. The key in the simulations is the material model and that is what I develop."

He seemed to grasp it, so then I asked, "You seem to know about this kind of stuff. Do you have a background in it?"

John answered, "No, but I do have a Ph.D. in Physics."

I inquired, "Where did you go to school?"

"I did my thesis work at Cornell under Carl Sagan."

"What was your thesis topic?"

"I studied cosmological issues, but the work never amounted to anything."

"Why not?"

"The timing of events was way off with current knowledge."

"What do you mean?"

"The age of the universe is known to be billions of years old, and my research showed much shorter time periods. Orders of magnitude lower!"

"But that is actually consistent with much of the non-radiometric data though." I went further, "Only the radiometric techniques date rocks with long ages. Other methods date the earth and solar system much earlier."

"What do you mean?" he doubted.

"There is much data available that indicates that the earth and our solar system is young. Radiometric halo studies performed by Robert Gentry when he was at Oak Ridge National Laboratories showed that polonium was generated in very short time periods in granite. Granite as you may know is supposedly the oldest rock on earth. This implies that granite was formed in a very short time span and not millions of years. Polonium dating methods have half-lives on the order of minutes, so we can experiment with the halo formation as the isotope transformation occurs."

I continued, "Another indication of a young earth is based on the calculation of Lord Kelvin, who argued for a comparatively short age for the earth. Based on Laplace's assertion that the sun spun off the earth, Kelvin assumed that the earth was white hot and calculated the solidification process as heat radiated from the surface of the earth. He calculated that if the earth were initially at this white hot state, we would have mountains at the equator on the order of forty miles high because of centrifugal forces. We don't see these altitudes at the equator, so the earth is much younger than the billions of years.

Yet another indicator of a young earth is the earth's magnetic moment. We are losing our magnetic moment every year. We have been measuring it for about 200 years now, and it is degrading. Russ Humphreys, a physicist at Sandia (Albuquerque), developed a theoretical model, called "The Dynamic Decay Theory" which shows that the earth is about only 6000 years old. This model was used to predict very accurately the magnetic moments of Venus and Uranus before Voyager 2 measured those planets magnetic moments."

The discussions continued in an animated manner, but I sensed that no headway was being made at all. As a matter of fact, John was hardening himself against me. I tried to have an ear to the Lord as I knew that God crossed my path with John's for some reason.

Although we both had backgrounds in science, I decided to drop the science issues and ask about his family in an appropriate break in our conversation.

I hit a nerve.

This bachelor was homeward bound. His dad had died within the last year, and he moved in with his mom in the D.C. area. That is why he took this job to work for the White House. He loved his dad and was still mourning his death. It was clear he loved his mom.

With a display of emotions he spoke, "My siblings have essentially ignored my mother, and they gave little consideration for my dad when he was dying."

His pain was clearly showing. I think it was mixed from his anger about his siblings and the bitterness of the loss of his dad.

"How many brothers and sisters do you have?" I inquired.

"One sister and one brother. They wouldn't budge to help my mom, so I had to move down here to take care of my mom."

He continued dumping his anger and feelings to me. I just sat and listened the rest of the flight as his pain seemed to dismantle the stoic look that I first observed when I first sat down next to him. While listening, I showed genuine concern for his soul, trying to listen and care for him as Jesus would.

As we finished our flight together, we exchanged business cards, and he thanked me for listening to him.

Before we stood up to leave I said, "My wife and I will be praying for you, your mother, and your siblings."

With a tear in his eye and with genuine graciousness he thanked me.

Apparently the reason that the Lord seated me next to this man was not share about what we had in common, science. But the Lord had something particular in mind that I wasn't aware of when I first applied for the first class upgrade. He wanted me to minister His healing to this man by penetrating into an area of hurt and pain.

I realized how much God loves this man and his family. He ordained this whole trip for me to sit next to that man to help him relieve some of his pain. I don't know if this was the first time that he shared his feelings with anyone. He didn't have a spouse to share these feelings with. I am sure that he has friends, but he was fairly new to the D.C. area.

In any respect, God wanted me there to listen to him and in the end to pray for him. That is all that is required of us by God sometimes. Although this man did not receive Christ as his Lord and Savior, he met with Christ in the flesh through me. Remember that it takes an average of seven path-crossings for a person to come to the recognition of the Lordship of Christ. God definitely ordained the seating arrangement on that flight. I trust Him to take care of John and draw him to Himself.

Something else should also be recognized here. When God orders our path to cross somebody else's path, we must be sensitive to the inner leadings of the heart. The heart is where the Lord directs us oftentimes. It is not necessarily what is in our heads. This is why we need to lay down our lives (and thoughts) for the Gospel's sake and obey his unctions and leadings that come from the inner workings of the heart.

Chapter 5 "The Storm"

Heb 12: 2 looking unto Jesus the author and finisher of our faith, who for the joy that was set before him endured the cross.... (KJV)

Nobody experienced as much as Jesus did when he was beaten, flogged, and emotonally barraged with spit and screams. The extreme persecution continued with his extreme loss of blood and hypothermia. Then finally he was crucified in the brutal Roman manner. Yet Jesus endured this treatment without cursing God the Father or man. How? You say because He was God. He was, but He laid that down and experienced all this pain as fully man. The nerves in his fleshly body felt pain that you and I would. His human body experienced the same limitation of sleep deprivation that you and I would have experienced. Every ounce of divinity was absent when darkness covered the earth for three hours while he took the sin of the world onto himself on the cross. Jesus exemplified his humanity when he cried out, "My God, my God, why have you forsaken me." It wasn't divinity on that cross; it was humanity. Yet he endured. How? It was the joy he imagined that he would experience after the pain subsided ... to see the victory over death, the grave, and hell. To be able to envision mankind free from these bondages is how he endured the long painful crucifixion. He focused on the future joy, not the current pain.

Joseph was also somehow able to see through his trials and foresee the end result before it happened. His brothers had thrown him in a pit and then sold him to traveling nomads never expecting to see him again. What was Joseph thinking? Was he upset? Was he bewildered? Was he discouraged? Was he angry? His response after meeting with his brothers years later reveals volumes: "you meant evil for me, but God meant it for good, in order to bring about this present result, to preserve many people alive." Somehow Joseph foresaw that God had a plan in the midst of that difficult situation. I am sure that the negative side of human emotion plagued him, but he showed no signs of bitterness or anger. When he saw his brothers again many years after they performed that wicked deed, he cried because he was so glad to see them. Joseph endured his cross for the joy that was set before him.

There is one aspect of my life where enduring the cross is difficult for me - when I am physically hurting. It is not as much of a problem if I am hurting emotionally. When it is physical, I have troubles focusing on the future joy and not the current pain.

On one of my flights, I came to understand the verse in Hebrews 12:2 in a deeper way. Not that I encountered even near the extreme pain that Joseph or Jesus endured, but I did experience their struggle in a small way. It was not a person who crossed my path on this flight but God. The purpose was to illustrate the depth of Jesus' pain as He died for my sins.

On the end of a job hunting trip just after I earned my Master's Degree in mechanical engineering at Ohio State University, my wife, Barbara, and I were traveling on a fairly small airplane from Roanoke, Virginia to Cincinnati, Ohio. We had an enjoyable time. The company that interviewed me paid for Barbara's travel, and the wives of the men that worked at this company had shown Barbara the area. This was the first interview Barbara had accompanied me. We were enjoying this whole new experience of interviewing together.

As we closed in on Cincinnati, the pilot mentioned that torrential rain mixed with snow was hitting the city hard. Within minutes Barbara and I realized that we were circling the airport and not descending. We weren't bothered but realized that we would be late arriving as we had to wait our turn to land. Little did we know that no one was taking their turn. The weather was so bad that the airport had stopped outgoing flights and encouraged the incoming flights to wait out the weather hoping it would pass by.

Barbara and I were not the least bit worried. We traveled enough to know that these kind of delays occurred. Then the plane started to drop. It seemed like a roller coaster dropping in the highest dip. It was unexpected. Suddenly I felt sick, nauseated to my stomach. Barbara was oblivious. She was looking out the window and actually enjoying the roller coaster. We bounced and tossed through the air. The pilot encouraged us, though a little late in my opinion, to fasten our safety belts. I believe we were the only people on the plane besides the stewardess and pilots. Barbara turned to me to hold my hand and tell me what she was seeing out the window. At this point, I was feeling faint as the up-and-down plane motion caused a sickness that I remember having at the amusement parks when I was a kid. I told Barbara not to touch me. I broke into a cold sweat. The stewardess was watching me and got on the loud speaker to mention that if "anyone" was getting sick, barf bags were in the pouch in front of us. She was looking straight at me since we were the only ones on the plane. The rocking and rolling continued, both with the plane and my stomach.

I breathed deep several times trying to focus on Jesus. I recalled the pain that he suffered in the Garden of Gethsemane waiting for his execution. His pain was not physical to start with although it ended up that way. *He endured.* His pain started in the emotional realm, waiting and enduring. I sensed a dichotomy within myself. A part of me was feeling faint, yet another part of me felt untouched and at peace. The furious battle that seemed to rage on the plane from the weather was similar now to the war of my weakened, frail flesh and my strong inner spirit. It's hard to explain. Deep within, you know that you are okay, but your body is reacting to the external circumstances. In a small way, this is what Jesus went through on the cross.

This path-crossing was not one of meeting another person, but one in which I met God in a new way. In the midst of this physical trial that I could not control, I sensed His presence. I couldn't seem to control my motion sickness. Though I couldn't change my body's reaction to the plane, I didn't panic, I just tried to focus on Jesus.

Within minutes (it seemed like hours) we were safely settled on the ground moving towards the drop-off gate. Barbara braved a few words, "Are you okay?"

I grinned back in a weak way, "More than you know." I still could not say much.

After my body calmed down a bit, I explained to Barbara what I was going through. When we got off the plane and into the airport, I posed a thought to Barbara, "There's no way we're going back into the air in this storm. We're renting a car the rest of the way to Columbus." As it turned out, we had a big plane and the flight to Columbus was uneventful, thank God.

As I reflected more on this occasion, I couldn't help but think how frail I was during that short trial. I don't remember ever going through a trial where Jesus immediately relieved me. In this case, I sensed His presence but no physical relief came. Actually, it did, but much later than I wanted. In comparison to the time and pain that Jesus had gone through from Gethsemane to the cross, my trial was just only a fraction of what Jesus experienced. However small it was compared to Jesus' pain, it was significant. I sensed the presence of God. I knew that He was present. Though my flesh was weak, I knew that He was there. *I endured.* That encounter I thought I would never forget.

Chapter 6 "The Scientist"

1 Tim 6:20-21 O Timothy, keep that which is committed to your trust, turn away from believing the profane and vain babblings of what is falsely called science, which some have erred concerning the faith. (KJV)

When the King James translators chose the word *science* in this biblical passage for the Greek word "to know," Sir Francis Bacon had already developed the scientific method about a hundred years earlier. But scientific endeavors had been around for a long time. In ancient Egypt, the diviners were the scientists. Aristotle had discussed scientific issues many years before Christ was born. When the Apostle Paul penned these words, Aristotelian "science" had been integrated into the Roman culture. Aristotelian science, now known to be wrong, did not include God. Timothy, the young believer, was aware of this Aristotelian science, and Paul was telling him that it is just "profane and vain babblings of what is falsely called science." There is much today that is falsely called science as well.

I sat next to a scientist, more precisely a physicist from Los Alamos National Laboratory, on my way to Los Angeles from Albuquerque who believed much of what I would term "falsely called science." No path-crossing could had been as strange as this one. He started the conversation by politely introducing himself, and we started with small talk. There was a tone in his voice that I couldn't quite pin down.

As the discussion continued, it became apparent that he was depressed. He had no family, and I wondered if he had any friends. He was a philosophical sort, open to other views but was struggling a bit with his beliefs.

At first he talked about science in metaphysical terms. In other words, there was a definite spiritual dimension to his philosophical belief system. He believed in evolution but agreed with me that there really wasn't much evidence for evolution.

He platonically stated at one point, "I recognize that evolution is only a philosophical framework to view the world."

He combined Darwinian evolution with some sort of new age god who is joined with nature almost in a pantheistic sense. In any case, it was confusing to me. I wondered if it was confusing to him as well, thus the explanation for his depression. As it turned out, it wasn't his confusion that caused the depression, but his belief in evolution. I never addressed his depression but tried to deal with the root cause. Our conversation went something like this.

"I am a scientist as well, but believe in the Bible and in Jesus as my Savior. I think that this is the most consistent, philosophical belief system there is."

"That's interesting, but how do you explain the data that evolution explains very clearly?"

"Like what?"

"Well, how about the fossil record? Fossils give indication that evolution has occurred."

"On the contrary, fossils actually prove that something catastrophic occurred in the earth's history. The flood of Noah's time in the Bible can easily explain the quick cover-up that is needed for the plants or animals to become fossils. It doesn't make sense that over millions of years that layers of rock covered these plants and animals, because decay and scavengers would not allow these materials to become fossils. But if sedimentation or rocks quickly covered up a plant or animal, then the dead animals could become fossilized."

I continued, "Furthermore, fossils show that animals and plants were in existence as fully formed creatures. There are no transitional forms. Here is what I mean. If cats became dogs, we would see one-quarter cats, three-quarter dog type of animals; we would see one-half cat, one-half dog animals; and we would see three-quarter cat, one-quarter dog kind of animals. We don't see any kind of these transitional forms in the fossil record. In fact, we see 100% cats and 100% dogs.

So to me, it is clear that fossils arc fully formcd plants or animals, but something catastrophically transpired in the earth's history that created these fossils. Darwin even recognized the problem with the fossil record and stated in 1859 that although intermediate fossils are missing, they would be found. It's been about 140 years, and still none have been found; so this lack of evidence speaks against evolution."

"So do you really believe in Noah's flood?"

"Yes, absolutely. I believe it, because the Bible says it. That is the basis of my philosophical belief system. Plus scientific evidences point towards a global flood event. Also, it is mentioned by most cultures in their books of antiquity. "

He seemed interested and did not give any signs of stopping the conversation so I continued. "There are marine fossils found on every mountain range in the world. How did they get there if water didn't put them there? With a global, catastrophic flood, these fossils are easily explained. The mountains, hills, and canyons also can be explained by a global flood view."

"It seems a little far-fetched to embrace such a view," he quipped.

I brought him back to the point that the scientific method requires that after an observation is made and a hypothesis is formulated about the observation, experimentation is then needed to withstand falsification before the hypothesis can become a theory or law. Evolution cannot be tested experimentally, because of the requirement for long time periods. No one has ever observed an evolutionary event to occur; *that* seems more far-fetched to me.

I continued, "Mount St. Helens produced many features that we see in geology today but produced them in a few days. A good example is that a canyon exists near where St. Helens blew. This canyon was produced by mud flows that eroded away the nearby rocky material. Afterwards, a stream ran through the canyon. The features resemble very closely those observed at the Grand Canyon. Although evolutionists believe that the Colorado River cut through the Grand Canyon over millions of years, the Grand Canyon more than likely developed by rapid mud flows with a river following afterwards just like Mount St.

43

Helens. Do you see that this is a recent 'experiment' that was observed by mankind? We can't experiment with the evolutionary belief, because the long time frames won't allow it."

His depressed, yet interested gaze encouraged me to continue, "It makes sense that a global flood which displayed catastrophic tectonic activity could have easily caused the Grand Canyon in the light of the Mount St. Helens observations. Do you know John Baumgardner?"

"No."

"He is a geophysicist at Los Alamos National Laboratory who has performed several calculations of that very same catastrophic event showing global flooding. He started with the Bible as his point of reference, similar to what I am explaining to you about my belief system. Genesis 7:11 states that the 'fountains of deep broke, and the windows of heaven opened.' He says that the fountains breaking up were portions of the lithosphere at subduction zones on the preflood continent. Some would liken it to Pangea."

My traveling partner knew that Pangea was the mass of land that included all the continents connected together. His nod of reassurance showed that he understood.

"Baumgardner's calculations based on the fundamentals of physics showed the break up of the continents in a very short time period and the resulting world wide flood. The oceans were superheated because of the lithosphere breaking up and the mantle head was released into the preflood oceans. The waters were heated so much they were spit up into the atmosphere causing global rain."

"I have not heard of that work," He paused and then continued, "he actually works on things related to the Bible? I guess some people are so committed to their belief, they'll even to work in those areas, like this guy."

"Aren't you committed to your belief system?"

"Yes, probably so much so it's to my detriment."

"Yes, I figured that."

I knew that this guy was caught up in the mire of a belief system that was causing his depression. He didn't see it though. It's hard sometimes to see those things in our lives. It's very healthy to step back somctimcs and cxaminc our actions. Our actions rcvcal what arc our beliefs. Actions follow belief, like effect follows cause.

I felt to ask the following question, "Do you believe in the after-life?"

"I don't know, but I believe as we evolve that we will evolve into a perfect being someday. This thought is prevalent in certain groups that I attend."

"But evolution does nothing for you now. You don't claim to be perfect do you?"

"No."

"Then there is the grave after which is nothing?"

"Yes."

"Well, I think that there is something after death, and the Bible is very clear about it. We are all destined to hell, because imperfection cannot get into heaven. We are imperfect creatures. The only way to heaven is to be perfect, but none of us can be perfect. Only Jesus was perfect. And His substitutionary death for us allows us access to heaven and into the presence of God. Jesus died to cover our sins."

"I will think about what you have said. After all, I know that evolution is just my frame of reference, but that is how I have been trained. After you have been trained for so long a certain way, it is hard to change. It takes time. And it takes a lot more information to think through all the issues."

After such a wise statement the only response that I could think of was: "Just know that I will pray for you."

He thanked me, and we went off into our little worlds probably each of us pondering the conversation that we just had.

I remember once talking to an atheist. I mentioned that if he really believed in evolution that he would commit suicide, because it is a purposeless, chance driven belief. It's only logical end was suicide, because if there was no purpose throughout a person's life then there would not be purpose on a day-to-day basis as well. He agreed and said that he had considered suicide many times.

I am reminded of the Bible verse that says the fool has said in his heart that there is no God. I am also reminded where Jesus said, "He who the Son sets free is free indeed." These folks with belief in evolution are subject to bondage that only Jesus can set free. Many times we can observe our actions; if our actions exhibit depression, bondage, lust, greed, or some other detrimental attribute then we should consider what our belief system is, that is, what is the root displaying this kind of fruit. Remember cause and effect, root to fruit, and belief to actions.

When we share the Gospel, we often miss the true root causes of problems in the person's life that we are witnessing to. We need to rely on God's Spirit to lead us to speak to the heart issues. For the physicist, he was depressed and it was because of his belief in purposeless Darwinian evolution. I am not saying that everyone who believes in evolution is a chronic depressant, but this fellow certainly was. Each individual is different. No matter where people are at, if we speak to root causes, we can then remove barriers to belief in God.

Chapter 7 "The Homosexual"

John 8:34-36 Jesus answered them, "Truly, truly, I say to you, whosoever commits sin is the servant of sin. And the servant abides not in the house forever, but the Son abides forever. If the Son therefore shall make you free, you shall be free indeed. (KJV)

"Do you really believe in absolute right and wrong? You can't legislate morality, you know," she parroted.

This was the confronting question that a gal and her friend who were sitting next to me on a trip from Oakland to St. Louis raised. They were in college headed home for a break from school. Dressed in earthy tones with ragged edges on their shirts and pants, the two pale-faced girls had engaged me in conversation with both barrels loaded. Without their knowing, the Lord had prompted my heart about their homosexuality and the painful background that one of them experienced. I didn't know the details, but deep down within my heart I knew that one of them had been sexually abused by a male authoritative figure.

I responded, "Let's consider the main issue of your question. The notion of moral absolutes."

"OK, let's do," one girl replied. "I believe in the theory of relativity. Because this physical law states that everything is relative and morals are relative as well. So someone can't tell me what is right and wrong. It's up to me to determine that."

"I believe in the theory of relativity, too. I am a scientist. I understand a little about gravitational time dilation and the issue with relative velocities and such. I even believe that it can be used for decisions in basic living as you mention. For example, when I get up in the morning, I don't think it matters if I use Colgate or Crest for my toothpaste. It is a relative thing to the individual. I respect that."

I continued, "But let's be consistent now in applying physical laws with moral laws in daily living. Do you agree that there are physical laws that are absolute? That don't change?"

"I am not sure. What do you mean?"

"Take gravity for example. It works all the time. You and I will come and go, but gravity has been acting, is acting, and will be acting. It is absolute and functions no matter what I believe about it."

"Well, of course, I believe in gravity."

"Then let's continue with this thought. Do you know anything about the Laws of Thermodynamics?"

"I know a little bit. They are related to how energy works."

"That's right. Thermodynamics essentially means how energy is transferred, the dynamics of energy. There are two laws. The first one says that energy cannot be created or destroyed. The second one says that energy is becoming less usable as it is transferred. The second law also says that as energy is being used, things become less organized or less ordered. In other words, things tend to go to disorder if left to themselves. Roads get potholes; bridges fall down; cars break down; and bath water turns from hot to cold over time. These are laws of nature, like gravity, that occur all the time, everywhere, and apply to everybody."

"I agree with those thoughts but where are you going with this."

"Well, just as you argued that some morals or decisions can be based on the physical law of relativity, so other morals and decisions can be based on the physical laws of gravity or thermodynamics. These are time tested laws that occur in your everyday life. If you jump off a bridge, because you don't believe that gravity will work, your belief doesn't really matter. You would fall every time and probably would die. It doesn't matter if you believe it or not. In a similar vein as the laws of gravity and thermodynamics are absolute, so are some moral laws absolute and always in operation. To answer your question. Yes! I believe in absolute right and wrong. Just like there are absolute physical laws like gravity and thermodynamics, so there are absolute moral laws. Furthermore, if you defy some of these moral laws such as trying to defy gravity, you will fall and eventually die."

"I understand what you are saying. I guess I have not thought about it like that. But what is an example of a moral law that is absolute and applies to everybody?"

"Again, I have to be consistent with my philosophical belief system which starts from the Bible. You see, God made both physical and moral laws. Johannes Kepler, a great scientist, said that all laws, whether physical, spiritual, or moral come from God. This is what I believe. And the Bible defines many of these laws. For example, the Bible calls sex before marriage fornication. The Bible also says that those who fornicate cannot inherit the kingdom of God. Now what does that mean? Well, God designed sex for a man and a woman in marriage. God didn't design sex for any other purpose other than heterosexual sex in the context of marriage. And he designed it for every age, every culture, and every nation. Everybody, all the time. When this law is violated, consequences occur. Now the consequences may not be immediate, but you can be sure that the cause and effect relationship that God designed regarding fornication will happen. God always wants the best for us and sex in a marriage is best for a person. Anything else is less than the best. "

"I don't believe that. First, I don't believe in God, and second, I think that sex is for people who love each other, whether they are heterosexual or homosexual. And I also don't think that they have to wait for marriage to have sex."

The answer kind of shocked me, but I didn't want to react to her comment, I just wanted to respond in a humble manner. I wanted her to continue, "Tell me about this God that you don't believe in, because I may not believe in him either?"

She basically portrayed God as someone ready to pounce on her for everything she did wrong. This I suspected came from her abuse at a younger age, imposing those feelings on any authority figure, including God. It was also interesting that in her description of God, she really did believe in Him although she said that she didn't. She was just terribly upset with Him and probably blamed Him for what had happened to her. I wanted to find out what happened to her.

I responded delicately, "Why do you believe that? Is it because that is what you want to believe or is it because something happened to you? Many times people justify their actions but really don't, deep down, believe what they are doing is right. I have had several foster children, and they act certain ways in reaction to the abuse that has happened to them. It's not that they necessarily want to behave that way, but they just do because of the sexual, mental, and physical abuse that has occurred. In turn, some of these people violate one of God's laws in reaction to something bad that has happened to them."

Pointing to the girl next her, she responded with kind, yet convicted words, "She and I are homosexuals."

"I knew that. I'll bet one of you, if not both of you, was abused by some male authority figure before."

"Yes, I was by my uncle."

In trying to be as sensitive as I could, I responded, "I don't mean to make light of what happened to you. As a matter of fact, I hurt for you. I have hurt for the foster children that my wife and I have parented. But when you, or I, or anyone have been hurt by someone, we have a choice to make. You can turn toward God or turn toward your own way. If you choose God's way, he can heal you. I have seen it happen. That is also very consistent with my belief system. The Bible is the object of my faith, and it says that Jesus died for my sins, my hurts, and my pains. He paid the price to heal me and heal you. That is love. That is true love. Taking on the pain so that someone else doesn't have to. But on the other hand, when you go your own way, you can get confused and go down a path that is destructive. Homosexuality is a sin as much as any other sin. It is not God's best for you, because you weren't designed for homosexuality. And it is destructive."

I paused for moment to allow for a response. None came. I wondered if she was hearing me or tuning me out. She may have been contemplating the abuse that occurred years earlier. Time went by. At this point, I didn't know what to say. I knew that God had spoken to my heart about these two girls, and that He loved them dearly. Since the airplane was on its descent, I knew I had about twenty more minutes for this path-crossing to end, so I decided to finish my conversation in a strong way.

"Please consider reading the Bible. You will find out about so much love that you have not experienced. I mean true love. Love is not just an emotional feeling. It is a strong act of a person's will. No greater love can occur than one would lay down his life for another person. This is what Jesus did when He died on the cross. He died so that you and I could have our relationship restored with God and understand and receive His love for you. His love can heal you. So much so, that you can be free from the fetters in life that chain you down. Jesus can brake those chains and give you true liberty. Liberty is not ability to do what you want to do when you want to do it. It is the ability to do the right thing all the time. The right thing is the best thing for you and the people around you."

Knowing that I unloaded on her I finished, "How does all that sound?"

She smiled and said, "Thank you. You are a kind man. At my meetings we learned that Christians were not reasonable people and hated us."

What meetings? I wondered. "Your welcome, but please consider Jesus as the center of your life."

She and the other quiet girl next to her both smiled and said that they would. I don't know if they were genuine in their response or if they just had enough of me. In any regard, they had heard some of the truth of God's word and if they applied it to their lives, it could make them free.

I also wondered over and over about that girl's statement about her "meetings." I don't know if she meant with other homosexuals or just with her homosexual friend. One thing I realized was that some people have an incorrect picture of God and of Christians. Maybe that is partially our fault. Many times path-crossings occur for us to shed a little light on people's skewed and hurtful view of God. I have heard it said that the only Bible that some people will read is my life.

And one last thing. I see it as our responsibility as children of God to share the truth of His love in a humble, not arrogant, manner. You are not better than someone who doesn't know God. You are just better off. God loves the homosexual as much as he loves you. The only difference is that you have received His love, and they have not.

Chapter 8 "The Sick"

Mat 4:24b ... and they brought him all sick people that were taken with different diseases and torments, those which were possessed by devils, those which were lunatics, and those with the palsy; and He healed them. (KJV)

If you read through the four Gospels, you will find references replete with how Jesus healed people as the verse mentioned above. It was the business of Jesus to heal peoples' emotional and physical pains. Jesus heals because physical ailments affect our spirits and souls. The apostle wrote in 3 John 2 that he prayed for our physical health to prosper even as our soul prospered. There is a direct link between our spirit, soul, and body. When one part ails, the others are affected. Most of us have experienced some kind of sickness in our lives. We can identify with the depressed feeling in our soul that follows when we are physically sick. God desires to heal us. That is why he put the self-healing capacity within the human body. Other inanimate materials don't self-heal, but the human body does. Sometimes the self-healing process of the body cannot overcome the sickness attacking though, for example, with cancer. At this time, God can heal supernaturally if he chooses. Our role is to pray for supernatural healing, but it is God's role to perform the supernatural healing. Another aspect of our role is to minister the sick person if God decides to let the natural self-healing process occur. This role demands patience and empathy, obvious characteristics of God, but many times lacking in us. That is what the next path-crossing is about.

The scriptures are not only filled with healing verses, they are filled with God's care and concern for children. God is even more concerned when a little one is sick. I experienced this first-hand on a trip from Washington D.C. to San Francisco when God saw fit to have a little sick boy cross my path.

I had been in difficult, tiresome meetings with a Navy research group that day. I presented research that encompassed about six months worth of work. My talk was in the middle of a day-full of technical presentations. I had to not only mentally review my talk but needed to pay close attention to the other presentations, because our work was very closely tied together. The audience had been polite but challenging at every turn. After my talk, I was tired and was looking to sit back and relax in a comfortable seat on the plane home. As a matter of fact, I wanted to just sleep. It didn't help that I suffered jet lag the day before and hadn't slept much the night before.

After stepping onto the plane, I remembered that coming to Washington D.C. I had a business class seat near the front of the plane. *Great! I will have more room to sleep on the return flight,* I thought. I glanced at my ticket stub, 25e. My seat was not in business class but in the back and right smack dab in the middle of this large plane. It was nine seats wide and my seat was not only the middle seat, but all around were swarming, loud children. My guess was that they were about eight to ten years old. I thought that there had to be mistake. They practically took up the whole section of the plane. How did I end up in the middle of this zoo? Shirts were flying overhead. Soft drinks were being passed back and forth. Food was being dropped everywhere. All this was happening, and we weren't even completely loaded yet to leave. This was not going to be a restful, peaceful trip. I thought, *This had to be mistake. Maybe I could get a seat somewhere else on the plane.*

Not a chance. The plane was full. Maybe if I closed my eyes, all the pomp-and-circumstance would go away. It didn't, and the continuing noise wreaked havoc on my nerves.

Yet in the midst of all the action and noise, I noticed that the boy next to me had his head laid in the cup of his hands. I was about to ask what group this was and where were they from but, instead, asked if he was OK. He was not all right, and I knew it.

"I feel a little sick," he replied.

"Your stomach or your head?" I asked.

"Both."

He was short with his words. I couldn't blame him. When I get sick, I don't want to talk either.

My thoughts were interrupted by the steward's voice, "Is he all right?"

"No, he is not feeling well."

"It's good you are here to watch him," he spoke reassuringly.

I knew that he thought I was one of the teachers or overseers or something, so I quickly responded, "I just met this boy. I am not apart of this group."

The stunned look on the steward's face showed agreement with my earlier thoughts. Surprised he said, "How did you get here in this pack of screaming, moving mass of children?"

"You got me. I was as surprised as you. I had business class reserved but somehow my reservation got messed up and my seat was given away."

I knew that there was nothing the steward could do to move me. The plane was packed full. Just minutes before they had asked for people to give up their tickets for those on stand-by. There was no hope of moving to another seat. I really didn't want to move anyway now.

Although I felt cramped in the midst of this sea of boisterous activity, I started to sense a God ordained plan. My mind shifted from all of the commotion toward God. *What do you want me to do, Lord?* I prayed silently.

I then realized that God placed me in the middle of the pack to care for that little sick boy. It wasn't a mistake that I didn't get into business class. It was God's plan. I had God's sense of purpose and peace now even amidst the noise.

During that trip, although not much was said between us, I tried to take care of this boy. When he was too weak to drink and eat dinner, I took the plate and cup from the steward and helped him eat. At one point, he started to get chilled, so I got some blankets and a pillow for him while in flight. In time, he fell asleep on my shoulder. I even prayed for God to heal him and restore his strength.

I felt cramped but felt the grace to embrace this situation. At one point, I noticed that the noise level had subsided. I don't know if it was because the lights were dimmed or because the energy ran out for these kids. Whatever the reason, I was relieved.

At the end of the trip, the boy thanked me as I handed him his back-pack. I assured him that it was no problem. Although I was still tired and a little harried from the trip, I could sense that I obeyed the Lord's direction by serving that child.

I did not witness openly to him about God's love for him. I just tried to show it. Maybe someday, someone else in his future will share the Gospel of Jesus Christ with him and the Lord will bring this occasion back to him. I don't know. Sometimes God calls us to be Christ in the flesh to people. He wants us to be His hands or His feet to those who cross our path. It is up to us to listen and to hear what the Spirit of God is saying in a particular situation. He knows what the people around us are going through. We don't. But, if we are sensitive to voice of God in our hearts, we can minister His love to those around us.

One thing is for sure. God cares for children, especially the sick. For Him to rearrange my seat and to transform my frayed nerves into a peaceful, calm was simply a supernatural event. All because of His love for that child.

Chapter 9 "Racism"

Gal 3:28 there is neither Jew nor Greek, there is neither
bond nor free, there is neither male nor female; for you
are all one in Christ Jesus. (KJV)

I passed the stewardess and looked toward my seat in 5C, the
first row after first class. Immediately I saw the man that would be sitting next to me. He was a large black man with what seemed like an
eternal smile. He was talking to two ladies behind him. As I turned to
sit down, he turned his attention towards me and greeted me with a
warm hello.

When I settled into my seat, I asked, "Are you from New
Orleans or Atlanta?" The plane was on its way to Atlanta from New
Orleans.

"I am from New Orleans headed for a pastor's conference in
Atlanta."

I shared that I was a Christian too, and he was excited. He
turned around to the two ladies, "There is a brother in the Lord sitting
next to me."

It was refreshing talking to him. We shared how we became
Christians, how long he was in the ministry, and several other issues
related to the moral state of the United States. Ends up, he was a pastor
in one of the largest churches in New Orleans. He asked about my job.
After finding out about my scientific background, he asked for my perspective on the relationship between science and philosophy.

In the midst of our conversation, something struck me, and I
realized it was the Lord prompting me. I was remembering what had
happened when I first came to Atlanta for my Ph.D. at Georgia Tech. It
was night time, and I was alone. Barbara stayed behind in California to
help my foster son, Bill, get set up for college. It was a long flight

across the country, and I was tired. Just before the plane landed, I looked out the window and saw Atlanta. Just as I was meditating on our new start in Atlanta, a thought ran through my mind. *Racism is a spiritual stronghold in Atlanta.* I knew it was the Lord speaking to me. Not an audible voice. Just an inner knowing, out of the blue. I knew that God told me that to let me know how I should pray for this town.

As I sat next to this black pastor from New Orleans, I decided to share with him the words that the Lord spoke to me on my descent into Atlanta. He was really intrigued by my story. I then asked him directly, "Have you had any experiences with racism here in the south?"

"Not really. Nothing other than a dirty look or nasty word once in a while. But I have had friends who have experienced it quite a bit. As a matter of fact, some of these guys are brothers in the Lord and still have the bitter experiences further damaging their perspective on white brothers in the Lord. This isn't right, but I understand where they're coming from." "I do too. I grew up in the North near Pittsburgh, Pennsylvania in a place called Weirton, West Virginia, and I have not experienced racism against me per se, but I have seen it. I can imagine how a bad experience could fuzzy up someone's view of how God wants them to look at people."

"That's right. It shouldn't be an excuse," he concurred.

"I think that the 12% difference of melanin in our skin is not the major difference in racism."

"You're right. It's cultural, man. I mean look at Bosnia. The war over there is cultural, and they have the same color of skin, yet there is a lot of racism going on."

He continued, "Another thing is that some black folks will call other black folks 'brother' when they don't know the Lord. A brother is not one of the same skin color, but one who has the same Father."

"I agree with that. When you know the Lord, the walls of cultural difference should fall down between us, because we are then in the same spiritual family. We have the same Father in heaven."

He began to teach me a few things about racism, "You know, racism is arrogance that comes from the world system, and as Jesus said we are not to live as part of this world although we live in this world.

Satan would do anything to cause division between black and white brothers as much as he would against brothers of the same color. Racism is just another ploy of Satan."

I had never thought of it like that before. He was right. Racism appeals to one's pride of being better than another. That is the way of Satan and caused his fall from God's grace. That is the way of the world! When the apostle Paul penned the words in Galations 3:28 of how God views no difference between Greek or Jew, or man or woman, which were inspired by the Spirit of God, he was confronting the cultural racism of his day. I had never thought of pride of mankind involved with racism, but it is clear. Before this statement, the women in all societies were treated as less important than the men. And in the Jewish culture, the Gentile was less important than those of Hebrew descent. But God values all people the same.

It is amazing that racism has been around a long time. It showed up in the story of Joseph when he was in Egypt. The Jews were coming into Egypt for food and looking for a place to live. They were viewed as a lesser people by the Egyptians, because they were another "people" who were shepherds. This was inherent racism at its core. From the fall of Adam, mankind has tried to raise himself up at the expense of another. Racism is one means to accomplish this perversion of what God intended.

Romans 5:8 says that He (God) is no respector of persons. This transforming Bible verse is a pivotal statement on the wickedness of racism – the elevation of one person over another because of race, creed, color, or sex. Even though the U.S. constitution states clearly that we should treat all men equal as God does, the fact remains that we do not. The notion about all men being created equal was in the U.S. and believed by most when at the same time slavery was a prosperous business.

Cultural racism is something I often ignore, but it needs to be addressed again in the Christian community in America as it has needed addressed in every culture down through the ages. I got a first hand reminder of that from this brother's path-crossing.

Chapter 10 "Perspective"

Isaiah 55:8-9 For My thoughts are not your thoughts, neither are your ways My ways, says the Lord. For as the heavens are higher than the earth, so are My ways higher than your ways and My thoughts than your thoughts. (KJV)

On a trip from Chicago to Baltimore I experienced an encounter with God that would change my outlook forever. It was night time and after spending a half day at work and then seemingly spending the other half in airports, I was tired. I was finishing the last leg of my trip into the Washington D.C. area. Being tired, I wasn't interested in completing my reading that I always enjoy on my trips, so I looked outside. The window seat allows such diversions from my usual planned reading during my flights.

It was amazing. I saw Baltimore, Washington D.C., and Philadelphia very clearly from their night lights. The light intensity was highest from the heart of each city and then gradually grew dimmer in a radial direction as I looked at the suburban areas. I was about 15,000 feet high on the descent and yet could see a span populated by millions and millions of people.

And then I thought about God's perspective. We are so caught up in our career, our home, our hobbies, our SELVES. We don't often see the big picture like I was viewing that night. What do these cities look like from where God sits? How big are they in His eyes? They must seem so small to Him. What about even states let alone the cities? Let's go a step further. What about the nation? The prophet Isaiah once wrote that the nations are as a drop in the bucket to the Lord. It seemed to me that the people in these cities were just a drop in the bucket or even smaller. God designed a very large universe and yet cares for each and every person on every continent, in every nation, in every state, and in every town.

He designed the world for us to inhabit, a place where He could lavish His love upon his created beings. This world which was designed from love is understood so clearly when considering the big picture.

Let me explain. Take for example your car. The engineers that designed the car considered the environment that it would exist in. They considered the hottest and coolest environments. They considered the potential extreme vibrations and shocks that the components would experience. On the basis of these various environments in which we call design constraints, the engineers designed the car for a specific life. When the car is not taken care of according to its design, it will not function properly during its life; furthermore, the duration of life will be reduced. We know of example after example of designed things that if they aren't properly used according to the design, the quality of life lessens and the time of life decreases.

Similarly, God has designed us for our environment as well. He placed the earth at just the right distance from the Sun. If we were a little further away, we would freeze to death. If we were a little closer to the sun, we would burn up. If we didn't have the earth's rotation, we would go unstable and perish. If the earth's tilt were not present, we would also experience more extreme temperatures that would cause imminent death. Considering all the constraints, God designed a perfect universe.

But just like obeying the engineer's design for the car, we must live according to God's design for our lives or it will not be lived according to the optimum design. Further, our life duration will inevitably be reduced. Just as the owner of the car must read the car manual to understand the maintenance of the car, so must we read God's manual, the Bible, for maintenance of our daily lives.

Another issue about design is that engineers know full well that many people won't read the car manual, therefore they design features into the automobile so that it wouldn't die instantly if it isn't operated perfectly. The same analogy arises when considering how God designed and created our world. He knew that mankind would sin.

Statistically speaking, if you have given free will to every human, someone is bound to choose to go against God. Of course, not just one did, but 100% of us did. None of us have ever operated under the perfect design. This is why Jesus was the Lamb slain before the foundations of the world. God knew that he would have to come in human form to redeem mankind. This is part of the design process though. A designer must consider how to make things work even though they haven't been used optimally. God is amazing in that he has thoroughly covered every base in design. His ways are truly higher than our ways.

Back to the view of the night overseeing the three cities, God cares for each individual in those cities, although they may appear to be insignificant. Certainly the people seemed insignificant in those cities from my view. Yet God cares. He cares deeply – so much that He gave His only Son for us to die for us so that we would not have to die eternally. Eternal life is part of His design.

It is only one aspect of God's design, but it is an important one: we were created for eternal life. Either living eternally with God or living eternally without God. This is why it is so important for us to share His love with others around us. He cares for them. He designed them. In fact, he designs path-crossings for His eternal purposes. He has purposes for each individual whether they are following Him or not. Some may be operating according to His design more precisely than others. Some are blatantly opposing the design for their lives. God saw this and knew it was going to happen. As part of His grand design, he devised path-crossings to allow those who <u>are not</u> operating according to the design to see the better life of those who <u>are</u> operating according to the design. It would do us well to see life from God's perspective, from the Designer's viewpoint. It is truly a life changing path-crossing when God interjects Himself into your life so that you can see the world from His perspective. That is more than just 15,000 feet above the ground. It is in the third heaven far above the world and its problems: *and you have been raised us up with Him and seated us with Him in heavenly places in Christ Jesus Ephesians 2:6.*

Chapter 11 "The Religious"

Mark 7:13 Making the word of God of none effect because of your tradition... (KJV)

There is very little that can make the word of God devoid of power. It was God's word that caused our universe to be created out of nothing. Jesus even said, "Heaven and earth will pass away, but my words will not pass away." They are everlasting. Eternal. When God speaks, something of permanence happens. Yet when Jesus confronted the Pharisees and Saducees, He stated that their religion would render God's word essentially powerless. Religiosity was substituted for relationship. How many countless times today do we see in America where religion is substituted for relationship? I was religious at one point in my life before I came to realize that I needed a relationship with the Lord.

When doubts come our way regarding God's love for us, we need to remind ourselves of what God has delivered us from. I had forgotten how God brought me out of religion into a relationship with Him, until He reminded me one day on a plane trip from San Francisco to Pittsburgh.

I was in first class for this night flight and was very grateful for the extra room that the first class seat afforded. The man sitting next to me was I am guessing about the age of fifty-five. He was a gray-haired, distinguishing looking gentleman dressed very formally in a suit and jacket. He was very friendly and started up the conversation.

"Hi! Is Pittsburgh your final destination or is it a transfer spot?"

"It's a transfer. I am headed to Cornell University in Ithica, New York."

"Are you a professor at Cornell?"

"No. I am a research scientist at Sandia National Labs in

Livermore, California and am working with a professor at Cornell. Where are you headed?"

He said with a smile, "Home!"

"Where is that?"

"In Williamsport, Pa?"

"Isn't that where the Little League Baseball Championships are played?

He responded with amazement, "Yes! I'm surprised that you know about that."

"Well, I played Little League Baseball and enjoy Major League Baseball a lot, so I have heard about it though I have never been there."

We continued the discussions on various topics and had a very enjoyable time. We talked about my foster son, Ross. After hearing about Ross' background and situation, he promised that he would send an official little league baseball to Ross. He kept his word as I received it several weeks later. He had talked very fondly about his wife and kids. He always looked forward to going home from his trips to see his family. At one point he mentioned that on many of his trips, his working buddies would go to lounges and bars and be unfaithful to their wives, but he chose the higher road valuing his wife more than these guys did. He also talked about the major league ballplayers who would send support to the little league office. It really was an enjoyable conversation with this man, who exemplified great moral attributes, genuine concern for others, and a generously giving spirit.

During part of the conversation, he mentioned something about his church. I asked if he was a Christian, and he nodded in agreement. But when I asked how and when he became a Christian, there was a look of bewilderment. He did not comprehend what I meant by the question. He thought he always was a Christian.

Nobody is always a Christian. We are born into this world with a sin nature and we are destined to hell unless some intervention occurs. This intervention is the ultimate path-crossing of life - a life changing meeting with Jesus. It is at this point, that a human must surrender his will to God's will. He must repent of his own ways and from being his own god. He must recognize that there is a power greater than he and that he is accountable to that power. That power is indeed the Lord Jesus Christ. Now some children grow up in Christian families and have prayed and talked to the Lord as long as they can remember. These people are genuine Christians, because they have an ongoing relationship with God. I am not referring to these kind of people here. I am centering on those people who never had a relationship with God although may have gone to church all of their life.

I knew that this man had not had a personal encounter with the Lord Jesus Christ by the bewildered look that he gave me. I realized Christianity was a religion to him. He probably went to church every Sunday. He was a good man. He was faithful to his wife. He was an honest worker, full of integrity. He loved his kids. And he was genuinely interested in me, a stranger.

But he was religious. In his life was religion, not a relationship with God, which gave him a false sense of security. I know, because I have been there. As we talked further, it became clear. He never had really given his life over to the Lord, nor did he have an ongoing relationship with the Lord.

This path-crossing reminds me of the type of religion that is commonplace in America. America claims to be a Christian nation, founded upon Christian principles. We indeed were founded on Christian principles by truly Christian men, but many Christians in America today are Christians in name only going to church and not having a relationship with God. Unfortunately, this amount of religiosity immunes one to the real need – a relationship with the Creator of the universe. This immunity also nullifies the power of God as it did when Jesus spoke. As such, our country does no longer operate under the power of God but under the whims of men and women who don't know the Creator.

Doing good things or obeying the ten commandments does not get you to heaven. We could never do enough good things to meet the perfection requirements that are needed to get into heaven. Sin is not allowed in heaven, not even one; God is perfect and to be with Him, you must be perfect. Obviously, we are not perfect. Even if we sinned only once a day, that would be 365 sins a year. If we lived 70 years, that would be a total of 25,550 wrong-doings. In any court of law, that would be enough evidence to convict a person. And that is a good person. Only one sin a day would be an earthly saint, yet that is not good enough to get to heaven. How can we get to heaven then, since we are not perfect? This is what makes Christianity different from all other religions. Religions are methods for mankind to reach God. They are bottom-up approaches. Buddhism, Islam, Mormonism, and "religious" Christianity. True Christianity recognizes that Jesus, who was a perfect human, sacrificed His life for the debt of our sins. It's a top-down approach. God left His place with all authority and power and became a man. Fully man, with every limitation. As a man, He walked perfectly and redeemed us with His own blood. The Bible says without the shedding of blood there is no remission of sins. When one turns from himself being the center of his life to God being the center of his life by asking for forgiveness, God then sees Jesus' perfection and not our own deeds – good or bad. Hence, the way to heaven, or into God's presence (it's the same thing), is by entrusting your life over to God by allowing the transforming life of Christ and the blood of Jesus to atone for your sins. This is what a true Christian is. It is transforming.

If you have never asked God for forgiveness and given your life over to Him; or never experienced this transformation; or don't quite understand what I am saying, you can start a relationship with God right now. Billy Graham, the great evangelist said, "you have heard it said, that seeing is believing; well, the truth is, believing is seeing."

Lay down this book and start talking to God just like you would to any human. Tell Him that you are sorry for sinning against Him. Tell Him that you want a new start on life. Ask Him to give you His promised comforter for your soul, which is the Holy Spirit. Do it now.

Now you are in a relationship with the Creator of the universe. Continue your relationship with Him by talking with Him all the time, not just on Sunday. This is praying. He is a friend that sticks closer than a brother. He is a God that delivers from all fears. He is one Who has infinite love to give you. He accepts you.

Besides praying, another important point is to read His word, he Bible. The Bible tells about His character and how to develop your relationship with Him.

Finally, get into fellowship with like believers, who have given over their lives to Christ the same way that you just did. If you do these three things – pray, read, and fellowship – you will grow in your relationship with Christ such that someday you will look back and not recognize the person that you are today. This would not happen if you were religious and going to church on Sundays, but will happen if you are in relationship with the One who made you. This indeed is the most important path-crossing that you could ever make.

Chapter 12 "Closure"

John 4:4 He had to pass through Samaria (KJV)

In the fourth chapter of John, Jesus left Judea for Galilee, his final destination. In the midst of his journey, He changed His route. Verse 4 states, "He needed to go through Samaria." This was not the shortest, most direct path to Galilee. It was His plan though. In Samaria Jesus went to Jacob's well. Verse 7 states, "There came a woman from Samaria to draw water." The disciples were gone at this time, so Jesus was alone with the woman. It was a divine appointment. God had destined that each of their routes through life would cross each other at this appointed time. The purpose of this path-crossing was for Jesus to share His love to her and to tell her about eternal life. She responded by believing.

The fundamental question underlying this book is: what is a path-crossing? A path-crossing is a special occasion by which two people intersect the other's journey through life for the purpose of one drawing the other, or both drawing each other, closer to God. It is an opportunity for Christ to be made known in a new dimension to a person. It is like the woman at the well meeting Jesus in John 4 or the unknown traveler meeting Joseph in Genesis 37.

Understanding a path-crossing is crucial to sharing the Gospel of Jesus Christ to unbelievers. Have you ever felt the urge to share God's love to your neighbor who was hurting didn't follow-through? Have you worked with your office-mate for years but never discussed your relationship with Jesus Christ? Are you aware of a family member that is not a Christian, and you have been afraid to approach him/her with the topic? To a Christian, the most important relationship is one with God through Jesus Christ, and we often claim that to our Christian brethren. However, God has called us to share our God-relationship with others, but many of us do not follow-through. If the peo-

71

ple that cross our paths don't know about our relationship with Jesus, then maybe Jesus isn't as important as we would like to think. Our actions truly speak louder than words. Imagine if Jesus didn't initiate the speaking with the woman at the well. She would not have known the Savior. Imagine if someone didn't share the Gospel of Jesus Christ with you.

Perhaps an illustration about friendships on the horizontal level would help motivate you to share the Gospel. I often think about how nice it would be if all my friends from West Virginia, Ohio, California, Georgia, and Mississippi could meet. If one of my friends from Georgia would plan on visiting me, I would be so excited to introduce them to my friends here. I would anticipate it. I would ruminate on it and prepare ahead of time. I would be excited about introducing them to each other. Now let's think about the vertical plane. Do I anticipate and prepare ahead of time about introducing Jesus to others? Am I excited about telling others about Him? Something is desperately wrong if I claim to be a Christian and am willing to share my horizontal relationships but not my vertical relationship with others.

This disparity, which occurs often in Christians' lives (and has in mine), arises for several reasons. One reason is that our vertical relationship with God is swamped by the horizontal, because our five sensory organs are inundated with information that desensitizes us to the spiritual dimension. We are so bombarded with things in this world that affect our taste, touch, smell, sight, and hearing, we fail to recognize the invisible things.

Another reason is because we don't understand why it is necessary for us to share our relationship with God to others. I wrestled with that for several years. The Bible is very clear about sharing the good news of the Gospel. But why? I finally understood when I thought about the time I first became a Christian. At that time I let everybody around me know I was a Christian. I was excited and unashamed. At times I was rude and impolite, so I tried to learn more tact. Over time, I became more tactful but seemed to have lost that original drive. What happened? Why does this phenomena occur so often? I believe it is because we have forgotten the bondages and death-filled life that God delivered us from. We have forgotten what we were like before we were saved by God's outstretched hand. Yet this is the very reason that we need to renew our commitment to sharing about God's love. These people around us are hurting and are in bondage to lusts, desires, and things that will eventually destroy some part of their lives or all of it. We need to have a renewal in our recognizing that people are going to hell.

It is for these Hell-destined people that God will put you across their path. He dearly loves them and is ever-reaching out to them. Just like he reached out to you through someone else. This time you can be the minister of reconciliation. Who are these people? And what do they look like? They may look great on the outside but on the inside, they are crying for help. They may be a family member. They may be a neighbor or co-worker. Or even be a stranger. They may be a Jew or a Gentile. They may be an atheist or homosexual. Wherever they are at in life, God has crossed your path with theirs so that you can interject Jesus' love and freedom into their lives. It is no coincidence or accident that certain people surround your life. Amidst human will, God sovereignly acts. God has put them there by design. He wants to free them from their bondages, heal their hurts, and change their course towards heaven.

Recall the words of Jesus long ago: The truth shall make you free. The motive for proclaiming the good news of the Gospel of Jesus Christ is to help set people free. We must not lose sight of this.

Proclaiming the truth because I want to but don't have to. This motto should guide us. Why? Because as people's journeys cross our paths in life, God wants to shine His life upon them. He reflects himself through us during these path-crossings.

The next time you are traveling on a plane, or visiting a neighbor, or working with a colleague, or vacationing in the Bahamas, remember that there may be someone whom God has ordained to cross your path. Prepare yourself for that. This is having your "feet shod with the preparation of the Gospel of peace." You never know. A person may cross your path someday whom you help to become the second-in-command of Egypt and even more importantly may become a child of God whom you see in heaven someday. Like the unnamed traveler in the story of Joseph, you may not be famous, but like him, you can forever change the course of someone's life and direct them toward God.